My Favorite Machines

Diggers

Colleen Ruck

A+

Smart Apple Media

Smart Apple Media
P.O. Box 3263, Mankato, MN 56002

 An Appleseed Editions book

Planning and production by Discovery Books Limited
Designed by D.R ink
Edited by Colleen Ruck

Library of Congress Cataloging-in-Publication Data

Ruck, Colleen.
 Diggers / by Colleen Ruck.
    p. cm. -- (My favorite machines)
 Includes index.
 ISBN 978-1-59920-674-5 (library binding)
 1. Earthmoving machinery--Juvenile literature. I. Title.
 TA725.R83 2012
 621.8'65--dc22

                         2011010309

Photograph acknowledgments
J.C. Bamford Excavators Ltd: pp. 14, 15; Shutterstock: pp. 5 (Marilyn Barbone), 8 (Anya Ivanora), 11 (Laurelie), 16, 17 (Tom Oliveira), 18, 20 (Robert Asento), 21 (Michael Zysman), 22 (Alexander Gordeyev); Terex Corporation: p. 13;

Printed in the United States of America at Corporate Graphics
In North Mankato, Minnesota

DAD0502
52011

9 8 7 6 5 4 3 2 1

Contents

Diggers Everywhere

A digger is a powerful machine for moving earth and rocks. It has big wheels so it can drive over rough ground.

This mini-digger can work
in very small spaces.

n the Cab

The cab is where the driver sits. It has big windows so the driver can see all around.

Levers steer the digger

Pedals swing the cab or arm right or left

The driver uses switches, **levers** and pedals to control the digger.

Loaders

Loaders have two arms at the front. A big bucket is attached to the end of the arms.

Arm

This loader is tipping out
its load of stone.

9

The Bucket

The bucket lifts and carries heavy loads, such as earth or **gravel**. This loader is carrying wood chippings.

Teeth

The bucket on this digger has teeth. They cut into the ground, breaking it up.

Excavators

An **excavator** is a digger with a long arm at the front. It can dig **trenches**, lift heavy objects, and carry earth in its bucket.

This is one of the biggest excavators ever built. It can lift more than 100 tons!

Backhoe Loaders

This digger has an excavator arm at the back. It is called a backhoe.

The driver can attach special tools to the backhoe instead of a bucket. This backhoe has a hammer to break rocks.

Hammer

Bulldozers

A bulldozer flattens and clears the **rubble** off a building site. The large blade at the front pushes the rubble into heaps.

Most bulldozers move on a pair of tracks instead of wheels. They can travel over bumpy or soft ground without getting stuck.

Making Roads

Before a road is built, the ground has to be **leveled**. A scraper has metal blades. They slice off the top layer of the ground.

When a road is almost finished, a paving machine moves slowly along it. It spreads a thin layer of hot **tar** and gravel.

Rollers

A roller drives along behind the paver. It flattens the hot tar and gravel to make it smooth and hard.

Special machines roll over garbage at **landfill sites.** They squash the garbage so it takes up less space.

Different Tools

Drill

This digger has a drill attached to it. The drill makes deep holes in the ground.

The grab on this digger
picks up and moves logs.

Glossary

excavator	A powerful digging machine.
gravel	Small stones used for making roads or paths.
landfill site	A place where trash is buried.
level	To make flat and even.
lever	A handle on a machine that you pull to make the machine work.
rubble	Bits of old brick, stone, and concrete.
tar	A thick, black, sticky liquid used for making roads.
trench	A long, narrow channel dug in the ground.

Web sites

www.jcbexplore.com
This digger web site is packed with fun games and activities.

www.kenkenkikki.jp/special/e_index.html
Learn how digging machines work.

www.pbs.org/wgbh/buildingbig/tunnel/challenge/
Take the "Tunnel Challenge" and find out about tunnel building.

Index

24